This book belongs to:

365 DAYS OF WONDER

{ Mr. Browne's Book
of Precepts }

R.J. PALACIO

ALFRED A. KNOPF
NEW YORK

THIS IS A BORZOI BOOK PUBLISHED BY ALFRED A. KNOPF

Copyright © 2014 by R. J. Palacio

All rights reserved. Published in the United States by Alfred A. Knopf, an imprint of
Random House Children's Books, a division of Random House LLC,
a Penguin Random House Company, New York.
Knopf, Borzoi Books, and the colophon are registered trademarks of
Random House LLC.

"Gracias a la Vida" copyright © 1966 by Violeta Parra

Visit us on the Web! randomhousekids.com
Educators and librarians, for a variety of teaching tools,
visit us at RHTeachersLibrarians.com

Library of Congress Cataloging-in-Publication Data is available upon request.
ISBN 978-0-553-49904-9 (trade) — ISBN 978-0-553-49905-6 (lib. bdg.)
ISBN 978-0-553-50996-0 (intl. tr. pbk.)
ISBN 978-0-553-50903-8 (ebook)

The text of this book is set in many different fonts and point sizes.
Printed in the United States of America
August 2014
10 9 8 7 6 5 4 3
First Edition

To Papi,
my first teacher

A teacher affects eternity;
he can never tell where his influence stops.

—Henry Adams

Precepts or maxims are of great weight;

and a few useful ones at hand do more

toward a happy life than whole volumes

that we know not where to find.

—Seneca

PRECEPTS

My father's name was Thomas Browne. And *his* father's name was Thomas Browne. That's why *my* name is Thomas Browne. I didn't know until I was a college senior that there was a far more illustrious Thomas Browne, who had lived in England in the seventeenth century. Sir Thomas Browne was a gifted author, a student of the natural world, a scientist, a scholar, and an outspoken supporter of tolerance at a time when intolerance was the norm. In short, I couldn't have asked for a better namesake.

I started reading a lot of Sir Thomas Browne's works in college, including *Enquiries into Very many received Tenets, and commonly presumed Truths,* a book that set out to debunk the prevalent false beliefs of the day, and *Religio Medici,* a work that contained a number of religious inquiries that were considered highly unorthodox at the time. It was while reading the latter that I came across this wonderful line:

We carry within us the wonders we seek around us.

The beauty and power of that line stopped me cold, for some reason. Maybe it was exactly what I needed to hear at that particular moment in my life, a time when I was racked with indecision about whether the career I had chosen for myself—teaching—was full of enough "wonder" to keep me happy. I wrote the line down on a little slip of paper and taped it onto my wall, where it remained until I graduated. I took it with me to graduate school. I traveled with the Peace Corps and carried it in my wallet. My wife had it laminated and framed for me when we got married, and it now hangs in the foyer of our apartment in the Bronx.

It was the first of many precepts in my life, which I began collecting in a scrapbook. Lines from books I've read. Fortune cookies. Hallmark card homilies. I even wrote down the Nike ad line "Just do it!" because I thought it was the perfect directive for me. You can draw inspiration from anywhere, after all.

I first introduced precepts to my students as a student teacher. I was having a hard time getting my kids interested in the essay-writing unit—I believe I had asked them to write one hundred words on something that meant a lot to them—so I brought in the laminated Thomas Browne quote to show them something that meant a lot to me. Well, it turned out they were much more interested in exploring the meaning of the quote itself than they were in its impact on me, so I asked them to write about that instead. I was amazed at the things they came up with!

Ever since then, I've used precepts in my classroom. According to *Merriam-Webster,* a precept is "a command or principle intended especially as a general rule of action." For my students, I've always defined it in simpler terms: precepts are "words to live by." Easy. At the beginning of every month, I write a new precept on the board, they copy it, and then we discuss it. At the end of the month, they write an essay about the precept. Then at the end of the year, I give out my home address and ask the kids to send me a postcard over the summer with a new precept of their own, which could be a quote from a famous person or a precept they've made up. The first year I did this, I remember wondering if I'd get a single precept. I was floored when, by the end of summer, every single student in *each* of my classes had sent one in! You can imagine my further astonishment when, the following summer, the same thing happened again. Only this time, it wasn't only from my current class that I received postcards. I also got a handful from the previous year's class!

I've been teaching for ten years. As of this writing, I have about two thousand precepts. When Mr. Tushman, the middle-school director at Beecher Prep, heard this, he suggested that I collect them and turn them into a book that I could share with the world.

I was intrigued by the idea, for sure, but where to start? How to choose what precepts to include? I decided I would focus on themes with particular resonance for kids: kindness, strength of character, overcoming adversity, or simply doing good in the world. I like precepts that somehow elevate the soul. I chose one precept for every day of the year. My hope is that the reader of this book will begin every new day with one of these "words to live by."

I'm thrilled to be able to share my favorite precepts here. Many are ones I've collected myself over the years. Some were submitted by students. All mean a lot to me. As I hope they will to you.

—Mr. Browne

Teach him then the sayings of the past,

so that he may become a good example

for the children. . . . No one is born wise.

— *The Maxims of Ptahhotep,*
2200 BC

JANUARY

We carry
within us
the wonders
we seek
around us.

—Sir Thomas Browne

And above all, watch with glittering eyes the whole world around you because the greatest secrets are always hidden in the most unlikely places. Those who don't believe in magic will never find it.

—Roald Dahl

Three things in human
life are important:
the first is to be kind;
the second is to be
kind; and the third
is to be kind.

—Henry James

No man is an island, entire of itself.

—John Donne

I yam what
I yam.

—Popeye the Sailor (Elzie Crisler Segar)

All you need is love.

—John Lennon and
Paul McCartney

The two most
important days in
your life are the
day you are born
and the day you
find out why.

—Mark Twain

Somewhere, something incredible is waiting to be known.

—Carl Sagan

To be able to look
back upon one's life
in satisfaction, is to
live twice.

—Kahlil Gibran

If the wind will
not serve, take
to the oars.

—Latin proverb

Don't tell me
The Sky's the
Limit When there's
footprints On
The Moon.

—Paul Brandt

How wonderful it
is that nobody need
wait a single moment
before starting to
improve the world.

—Anne Frank

However
long the
night ...
the dawn
will
break.

—African proverb

He who knows
others is clever,
but he who knows
himself is
enlightened.

—Lao Tzu

the
best
way to
make
your

dreams come true is to wake up.

—Paul Valéry

Just be who
you want
to be,
not what
others
want to see.

—Unknown

NOT
ALL THOSE
WHO WANDER
ARE LOST

—J.R.R. Tolkien

Make kindness your
daily modus operandi and
change your world.

—Annie Lennox

You are braver than you
believe, stronger than you seem,
and smarter than you think.

—Christopher Robin (A. A. Milne)

Have you
had a
kindness
shown?
Pass it on.

—Henry Burton

Don't dream it, be it.

—*The Rocky Horror Picture Show*

The miracle
is not to fly in
the air, or
to walk on the
water, but
to walk on the
earth.

—Chinese proverb

There is no shame in not
knowing. The shame lies
in not finding out.

—Assyrian proverb

To thine own self be true.

—William Shakespeare

No act of
kindness,
no matter
how small,
is ever
wasted.

—Aesop

Be yourself,
Everyone Else is
already taken.

—Oscar Wilde

Wherever there is a
human being there
is an opportunity
for a kindness.

—Seneca

Know thyself.

—Inscription at the Oracle of Delphi

Laughter
is sunshine;
it chases
winter
from the
human face.

—Victor Hugo

The future belongs to those who believe in the beauty of their dreams.

—Eleanor Roosevelt

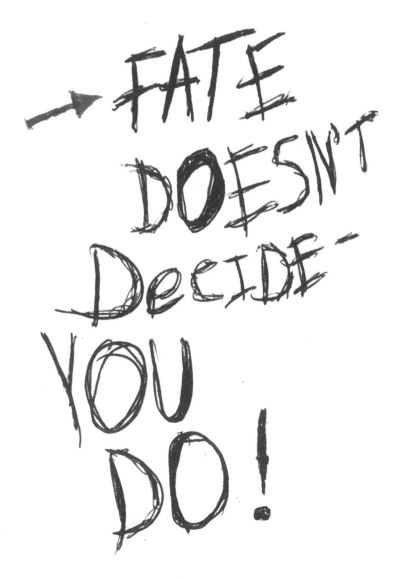

FATE DOESN'T DECIDE— YOU DO!

—Dominic

H ere's a secret, kids: parents spend a lot of time teaching you how to be polite when you're very young because, it's a scientific fact, the world is nicer to polite people. *"Don't forget to say please,"* we tell you. *"Play nice. Say thank you."* These are elemental virtues. We teach them because they're good things to teach. And we want people to like you.

By the time you guys get to middle school, though, our priorities seem to shift. *"Do well in school. Succeed. Study harder. Have you finished your homework yet?"* That's what we tend to harp on then. Somewhere along the way, we stop emphasizing those elemental virtues. Maybe it's because we assume you've learned them by now. Or maybe it's because we've got so many other things we want you to learn. Or maybe, just maybe, it's because there's an unwritten law about middle-school kids: it's hard to be nice. The world may prefer polite children, but other middle schoolers don't seem to really appreciate them. And we parents, eager to see you guys get through these *Lord of the Flies* years, often turn a blind eye to some of the mean stuff that passes for normal.

I personally don't buy this notion that all kids go through a "mean phase." In fact, I think it's a lot of malarkey! Not to mention a little insulting to kids. When I talk to parents who tell me, as a way of justifying something unkind their child has done, "What can I do? Kids will be kids," it's all I can do not to bop them on their heads with a friendship bracelet.

Here's the thing: with all due respect, guys, I don't think you're always equipped to figure things out on your own. Sometimes there's a lot of unnecessary meanness that happens while you're trying to sort out who you want to be, who your friends are, who your friends are not. Adults spend a lot of time talking about bullying in schools these days, but the real problem isn't as obvious as one kid throwing a Slurpee in another kid's face. It's about social isolation. It's about cruel jokes. It's about the way kids treat one another. I've seen it with my own eyes, how old friends can turn against each other: it seems, sometimes, that it's not enough for them to go their separate ways—they literally have to "ice" their old buddies out just to prove to the new friends that they're no longer still friends. That's the kind of stuff I don't find acceptable. Fine, don't be friends anymore: but stay kind about it. Be respectful. Is that too much to ask?

Na-hah. I don't think so.

Every day at 3:10 p.m., my fifth graders stream out of Beecher Prep at dismissal time. A few of you, the ones who live nearby, walk home. Some of you take a bus or the subway. A lot of you, though, are picked up by parents or caregivers. The point is, either way, most parents don't allow their kids to roam around the city without knowing where they are, who they're with, and what they're doing. Why is that? Because you're still kids! So why should we let you roam wild in the uncharted territory of middle school without just a little bit of guidance? You're asked to navigate social situations every day—lunchroom politics, peer pressure, teacher relations. Some of you do it very well on your own, absolutely! But others—and let's be honest here—don't. Some of you still need a little help figuring things out.

So, kids, don't get mad at us if we try to help you in this regard. Be patient with us. It's always tricky, as a parent, striking the right balance between too much intervention and too little. So bear with us. We're only trying to help. When we remind you about those old, elemental virtues we used to teach you back in your toddler days, when you were still playing in sandboxes, it's because "playing nice" is something that doesn't end when you start middle school. It's something you need to remember every day as you walk through the school hallways on your way to becoming adults.

The truth of the matter is this: there's so much nobility lurking inside your souls. Our job as parents, and educators, and teachers, is to nurture it, to bring it out, and to let it shine.

—Mr. Browne

FEBRUARY

It is better
to ask
some of the
questions
than to know
all the
answers.

—James Thurber

I expect to pass through
this world but once.
Any good, therefore,
that I can do or any
kindness I can show
to any fellow creature,
let me do it now.
Let me not defer or
neglect it, for I
shall not pass this
way again.

—Stephen Grellet

The supreme happiness
of life is the conviction
that we are loved.

—Victor Hugo

Love
a little
more
each day.

—Madison

Give me a firm
place to stand,
and I will move
the earth.

—Archimedes

I am an
expression
of the
divine.

—Alice Walker

If you ever
feel lost,
let your
heart
be your compass.

—Emily

Everything
you can
imagine
is real.

—Pablo Picasso

If thou follow
thy star, thou
canst not fail of
glorious haven.

—Dante Alighieri

Find Your GREATNESS

—Rebecca

We all have the same roots,
and we are all branches of
the same tree.

—Aang (*Avatar: The Last Airbender*)

Man can learn
nothing unless he
proceeds from
the known to the
unknown.

—Claude Bernard

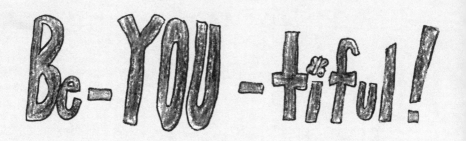

—Lindsay

To be loved, be lovable.

—Ovid

The smile is the shortest distance between two persons.

—Victor Borge

Those who try to do
something and Fail
are infinitely better
than those who try
to do nothing and
succeed.

—Lloyd Jones

Every time the Sun rises,

A NEW

HOPE Begins...

—Jack

The main thing is
to be moved, to love,
to hope, to tremble,
to live.

—Auguste Rodin

The greatest
glory in living
lies not in
never falling,
but in rising
every time
we fall.

—Nelson Mandela

Whatever you are, be a good one.

—Abraham Lincoln

Don't tell me not to fly, I've simply got to.

—Bob Merrill and Jule Styne,
"Don't Rain on My Parade"

Kindly words
do not enter
so deeply into
men as a
reputation
for kindness.

—Mencius

Hard work
beats talent
when talent
doesn't work
hard ☺

—Shreya

Keep a green tree in your heart
and a singing bird may come.

—Chinese proverb

They are
never alone
that are
accompanied
with noble
thoughts.

—Sir Philip Sidney

When you come to the
end of your rope, tie a
knot in it and hang on.

—Thomas Jefferson

It's not what
happens to you,
but how you react
that matters.

—Epictetus

For
kindness
begets
kindness
evermore.

—Sophocles

I like including a precept about discovery at this time of year. Why this time of year? Because, although February is the shortest month, it also happens to be the longest stretch of time without an event to look forward to (Presidents' Day notwithstanding). In January, students have just come off the holiday high that is December. With the rush of presents and the thrill of the first few snowfalls behind them, by January 31 the realization hits: "We won't have another big stretch of vacation time until spring break!" Argh! Hence: the February doldrums.

I've always found that it helps to get my students thinking about unexplored frontiers—be they frontiers of the imagination or geographical frontiers. The latter dovetail nicely with what they're usually doing in history at this time of year (exploring either ancient China or ancient Greece, depending on their history teacher), and the former are a great segue into my Creative Writing unit.

I recently used the James Thurber precept "It is better to ask some of the questions than to know all the answers" and got a really interesting essay back from a student named Jack Will.

I like this precept a lot a lot a lot. It makes me think about all the stuff I don't know. And maybe never, ever will know. I spend a lot of time asking myself questions. Some are stupid questions. Like, why does poop smell so bad? Why don't human beings come in as many shapes and sizes as dog breeds do?

(I mean, a mastiff is like ten times bigger than a Chihuahua, so why aren't there humans who are sixty feet tall?) But I also ask myself bigger questions. Like, why do people have to die? Why can't we just print more money and give it to people who don't have enough of it? Stuff like that.

So, the big question I've been asking myself a lot this year is, why do we all look the way we do? Why do I have one friend who looks "normal" and another friend who doesn't? These are the kinds of questions that I don't think I'll ever know the answers to. But asking myself the questions did make me ask myself another question, which is, what is "normal" anyway?

So I looked it up in oxforddictionaries.com. This is what it said:

normal (adjective): Conforming to a standard; usual, typical, or expected.

And I was like, "conforming to a standard"? "Usual? Typical? Expected?" Ugh! Who the heck wants to be "expected" anyway? How lame is that?

So that's why I really like this precept.

Because it's true! It's better to ask some really awesome questions than it is to know a lot of dumb answers to stupid stuff. Like, who cares what x equals in some dumb equation? Duh! Answers like that don't matter! But the question "What is normal?" does matter! It matters because there's never going to be a right answer. And there's no wrong answer, either. The question is all that matters!

This is why I love using precepts in my classroom. You throw them out there, and you never know what you're getting back, what's going to strike a chord with a kid, or what's going to make them think a little deeper, a little bigger, than if they were just trying to answer a question from a book. It's one of the things I love most about precepts: the sentiments they voice are usually about things that human beings have been grappling with since the dawn of time. I love that my fifth graders are doing the same!

—Mr. Browne

MARCH

Kind words do not cost much. Yet they accomplish much.

—Blaise Pascal

Never doubt that
a small group of
thoughtful, committed
citizens can change
the world.
Indeed, it's the
only thing that ever has.

—Margaret Mead

To me, every hour of

the light and dark

is a miracle,

Every inch

of space is a miracle.

—Walt Whitman

How like an Angel came I down!

—Thomas Traherne

Superheroes are made but heroes are born.

—Antonio

A tree is known by its
fruit; a man by his deeds.
A good deed is never lost;
he who sows courtesy
reaps friendship, and
he who plants kindness
gathers love.

—St. Basil

Do not go where
the path may
lead, go instead
where there is no
path and leave
a trail.

—Ralph Waldo Emerson

Life is a ticket to
the greatest show
on earth.

—Martin H. Fischer

To know what
you know and
what you do not
know, that is
true knowledge.

—Confucius

Happiness is not something ready-made. It comes from your own actions.

—Dalai Lama

Always do right. This will
gratify some people and
astonish the rest.

—Mark Twain

That Love is all there is,
Is all we know of Love.

—Emily Dickinson

What lies behind us
and what lies before
us are but tiny matters
compared to what lies
within us.

—Henry Stanley Haskins

Thousands of candles can be lit from a single candle, and the life of the single candle will not be shortened. Happiness never decreases by being shared.

—Bukkyo Dendo Kyokai,
The Teaching of Buddha

Paradise on Earth is where I am.

—Voltaire

In this world, one needs
to be a little too good in order
to be good enough.

—Pierre Carlet de Chamblain de Marivaux

Good actions are the
invisible hinges on the
doors of heaven.

—Victor Hugo

Be the person
who can smile
on the
worst day.

—Cate

Don't just go
with the flow,
take some
dares through
the rapids.

—Isabelle

Where there
is love, there
is joy.

—Mother Teresa

Hope is like the Sun.

When it's behind the clouds, it's not gone. YOU just have to FIND it!

—Matthew

your
best
takes
your
time.

—Thomas

What wisdom can you find that is greater than kindness?

—Jean-Jacques Rousseau

MARCH 24

The man who moves a
mountain must start by
moving small stones.

—Chinese proverb

You can do anything you want. All you have to do is Believe

—Ella

Be kind whenever
possible. It is always
possible.

—Dalai Lama

As soon as you trust yourself,
you will know how to live.

—Johann Wolfgang von Goethe

We must dare,
dare again,
and go on
daring!

—Georges Jacques Danton

No bird soars too high if he
soars with his own wings.

—William Blake

Life is about using the whole box of crayons.

—RuPaul

Life is like a rollercoaster...

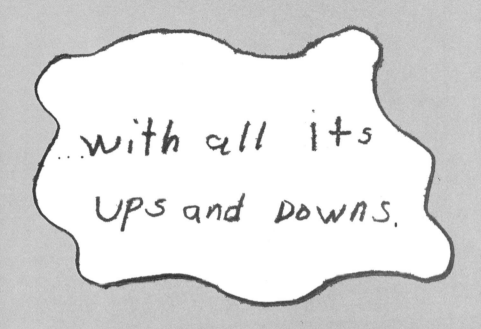

...with all its ups and Downs.

—Kyler

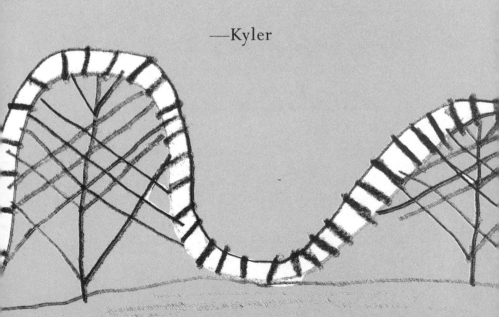

When Tommy, my son, was three years old, my wife, Lilly, and I took him for his annual checkup and the pediatrician asked us what his eating habits were like.

"Well," we confessed, "he's going through this phase of only liking chicken fingers and carbs, so we've kind of given up trying to get him to eat vegetables for now. It's become too much of a struggle every night."

The pediatrician nodded and smiled, and then said, "Well, you can't really force him to eat the veggies, guys, but your job is to make sure they're on his plate. He can't eat them if they're not even on his plate."

I've thought about that a lot over the years. I think about it with teaching. My students can't learn what I don't teach them. Kindness. Empathy. Compassion. It's not part of the curriculum, I know, but I still have to keep dishing it out onto their plates every day. Maybe they'll eat it; maybe they won't. Either way, my job is to keep on serving it to them. Hopefully, a little mouthful of kindness today may make them hungry for a bigger taste of it tomorrow.

—Mr. Browne

APRIL

What is beautiful is good, and who is good will soon be beautiful.

—Sappho

'Tis always
morning
somewhere in
the world.

—Richard Henry Hengist Horne

Knowledge, in truth, is the great sun in the firmament. Life and power are scattered with all its beams.

—Daniel Webster

Nothing can make our life, or the lives of other people, more beautiful than perpetual kindness.

—Leo Tolstoy

—Delaney

Be the change
you want to see
in the world.

—Mahatma Gandhi

Life can only be understood
backwards; but it must be
lived forwards.

—Søren Kierkegaard

Heaven is under our feet as well as over our heads.

—Henry David Thoreau

Be noble! and the nobleness that lies

In other men, sleeping but never dead,

Will rise in majesty to meet thine own.

—James Russell Lowell

He was a bold man that first ate an oyster.

—Jonathan Swift

It's not whether
you get knocked down,
it's whether you get up.

—Vince Lombardi

The world is good-natured
to people who are
good-natured.

—William Makepeace Thackeray

The
universe
is what
you illustrate
it to be.

—Rory

The difference
between ordinary
and extraordinary
is that little extra.

—Jimmy Johnson

I am only one,

But still I am one.

I cannot do everything,

But still I can do something;

And because I cannot do everything,

I will not refuse to do the something that I can do.

—Edward Everett Hale

You can complain because roses have thorns, or you can be grateful because thorn bushes have roses.

—Ziggy (Tom Wilson)

Use what talent you possess: the woods would be very silent if no birds sang except those that sang best.

—Henry van Dyke

The goal of life is to make
your heartbeat match the
beat of the universe, to match
your nature with Nature.

—Joseph Campbell

Even the
toughest
Dogs can
be afraid
of vacuums.

—Anna

Do a deed of
simple kindness;
though its end
you may not see,
it may reach, like
widening
ripples, down a
long eternity.

—Joseph Norris

We love the things we love for what they are.

—Robert Frost

APRIL 22

Ideals are like stars; you will not
succeed in touching them with your
hands. But like the seafaring man
on the desert of waters, you choose
them as your guides, and following
them you will reach your destiny.

—Carl Schurz

You don't live in a world all alone.

Your
brothers
are here,
too.

—Albert Schweitzer

I feel no need for
any other faith than my faith
in human things.

—Pearl S. Buck

Today I have grown
taller from walking
with the trees.

—Karle Wilson Baker

The great man does not think
beforehand of his words that they
may be sincere, nor of his actions
that they may be resolute—he simply
speaks and does what is right.

—Mencius

Wherever you are it is your own friends who make your world.

—William James

There are
many great
deeds
done in
the small
struggles
of life.

—Victor Hugo

Don't wait until you know
who you are to get started.

—Austin Kleon

To each, his own is
beautiful.

—Latin proverb

My grandparents were avid Scrabble players. They played every night, whether they had company or not—on the same Scrabble board they'd had for over fifty years. Their matches were formidable because they were both incredible players. Interestingly, my grandfather, who was known in my family as being the "intellectual," almost always lost to my grandmother. It's not that Grandma wasn't every bit as smart as Grandpa, by the way—it's just that he was the one who had gotten a degree at Columbia while Grandma stayed home to raise my mother and her sisters. Grandpa was a lawyer, and Grandma was a homemaker. Grandpa had a library of books, and Grandma liked doing crosswords. Grandpa hated to lose, and Grandma whipped his butt nine out of every ten games for over fifty years.

One time I asked Grandma what her secret to winning was, and she said, "It's simple. Just play your tiles."

"Okay, Grandma, a little elaboration is needed here," I answered.

"Here's why I always beat your grandfather. He hoards his tiles. When he gets good letters, he holds on to them, waiting to play them on a triple-word score. He'll skip a turn to try and get a seven-letter word to get the fifty-point bonus. Or he'll trade in his letters in the hope he'll get better ones. That's no way to play!"

"It's his strategy," I said, trying to defend him.

She waved her hand in the air dismissively. "Me, I just play my tiles—whatever tiles I get. Doesn't matter if they're good letters or bad letters. Doesn't matter if they're on a triple-word score or not. Whatever tiles I get, I play. I make the most of them. That's why I always beat your grandpa."

"Does he know this?" I asked. "Haven't you ever shared this secret with him?"

"What secret? He's watched me play every night for fifty years—do you think my way of playing is a secret? Play the tiles you get! That's my secret."

"Grandpa," I said later to my grandfather. "Grandma told me the reason she always beats you at Scrabble is because she always plays her tiles and you hold on to yours. Have you ever thought about changing your style of playing a bit? Maybe you would win more often!"

Grandpa poked his finger into my chest. "That's the difference between your grandma and me," he answered. "I want to win, but only if I can win beautifully. Big, long words. Words no one's ever heard of before. That's me. Your grandmother, she's fine winning with nothing but a string of A's and O's. You know the old saying: *Suum cuique pulchrum est!* To each, his own is beautiful."

"That may be true, Grandpa, but Grandma's kicking your butt!" I said.

Grandpa laughed. *"Suum cuique pulchrum est!"*

—Mr. Browne

MAY

MAY 1

Play the tiles you get.

—Grandma Nelly

Do all the good you can,
By all the means you can,
In all the ways you can,
In all the places you can,
At all the times you can,
To all the people you can,
As long as you ever can.

—John Wesley

There is nothing
stronger in the world
than gentleness.

—Han Suyin

MAY 4

A single act of kindness throws
out roots in all directions, and
the roots spring up and make
new trees.

——Father Faber

Winners never quit and quitters never win

—Vince Lombardi

Cherish that which is
within you.

—Chuang Tzu

Follow your dreams.
It may be a long
journey, but the
path is right in
front of you.

—Grace

It's not the load that
breaks you down.
It's the way you carry it.

—*C. S. Lewis*

Though we travel the world over to find the beautiful, we must carry it with us or we find it not.

—Ralph Waldo Emerson

The breeze at dawn has
secrets to tell you.
Don't go back to sleep.

—Rumi

IF PLAN "A" DOESN'T
WORK, JUST REMEMBER:
THE ALPHABET HAS
25 MORE LETTERS.

—Unknown

The world does not
know how much it
owes to the common
kindnesses which so
abound everywhere.

—J. R. Miller, *The Beauty of Kindness*

The best and most
beautiful things in
the world cannot be seen
or even touched.
They must be felt with
the heart.

—Helen Keller

You were born An original. don't become a copy.

—Dustin

FIND THINGS THAT SHINE AND MOVE TOWARD THEM.

—Mia Farrow

If you want to be
well-liked, you got
to be yourself.

—Gavin

If your
ship doesn't
come in,
swim out
to it.

—Jonathan Winters

All we are saying is give
peace a chance.

—John Lennon

The purpose of life is a
life of purpose.

—Robert Byrne

Believe in life!

—W.E.B. Du Bois

You're free to make your own choices, but you will never be free of the CONSEQUENCES of your choices.

—Srishti

Making a million friends is not
a miracle . . . the miracle is to
make such a friend who can
stand with you when millions
are against you.

—Unknown

Have I done an unselfish thing?
Well then, I have my reward.

—Marcus Aurelius

The wind is blowing.
Adore the wind!

—Pythagoras

The chief
happiness
for a man
is to be
what he is.

—Desiderius Erasmus

A single conversation
across the table with a wise
man is worth a month's
study of books.

—Chinese proverb

Your actions are all
you can own.

——Flynn

Just love life
and it will love
you back

—Madeline

Kindness is a language the deaf can hear and the blind can see.

—Mark Twain

Is it so small a thing
To have enjoyed the sun,
To have lived light
in the spring,
To have loved, to have
thought, to have done;
To have advanced true
friends, and beat
down baffling foes?

—Matthew Arnold

a multitude of small

delights constitute

happiness.

—Charles Baudelaire

Every now and again I have to remind my students that they're not invisible. "I can see you rolling your eyes!" I tell them. They think this is funny—usually. And it is—usually. But the other night I was reminded of how easy it is for kids to forget that their actions are, indeed, noted.

I was attending the upper-school play at Beecher Prep and took a seat next to the mother of one of my former students, whom I'll call Briana. This was a sweet, bright girl who had experienced some difficulties with a group of mean girls in middle school. Briana was shy and a little awkward, so I was surprised when her mom told me that she'd been cast in the lead role of the play. Her mom was so proud! She said that her daughter had really come out of her shell in upper school, due largely to the recognition she'd gotten for her singing and acting talent.

When the play started, the moment Briana came onstage, I understood what her mom meant. Gone was that awkward little girl I remembered from fifth grade, replaced by a very confident leading lady who could easily have been mistaken for a young Nicole Kidman. "Good for you, Briana!" I thought to myself. But no sooner had she finished singing her first verse than I noticed, sitting a couple of rows in front of us, those same three girls who used to taunt her in middle school. None of them even went to the school anymore (they hadn't been accepted to the upper school largely because of the school's strong anti-bullying commitment). These girls snickered the moment Briana came onstage. They whispered to one another behind open hands. I'm sure they didn't think anyone was noticing them, but I could see out of the corner of my eye that Briana's mom saw everything as clearly as I did. I can't even describe the look on her face. It was heartbreaking.

I waited for Briana to finish her solo. The moment the applause started, I leaned over the seat in front of me and tapped the shoulder of one of the girls. She turned around and started to smile when she saw me, but then she noticed my expression as I mouthed the words *Shut up!* The other girls saw this, too.

I think the shock of seeing Mr. Browne, their formerly mellow English teacher, so angry, using language that he had never used with them before, had its intended effect: they were quiet as church mice for the rest of the first act. During intermission, they quickly disappeared and didn't come back for Act Two.

By the time the play ended, I had almost forgotten about those idiotic girls amid the thunderous applause. I turned to Briana's mom to congratulate her on her daughter's truly brilliant performance. She was smiling, but there were tears in her eyes. I don't know if they were tears of pride or if there was a trace of bitterness over the fact that those girls had marred what should have been a completely joyful night for her. All I know is that my memory of those girls will be forever altered by their thoughtless behavior that night. I'm sure they didn't mean for Briana's mom to see them, but it doesn't matter. Your actions are noted, kids. And remembered.

—Mr. Browne

JUNE

Just follow the day and reach for the sun!

—The Polyphonic Spree

Ignorance is not
saying, I don't know.
Ignorance is saying,
I don't want to know.

—Unknown

Start by doing
the necessary,
then the possible,
and suddenly
you are doing
the impossible.

—St. Francis of Assisi

Don't worry about a thing
'cause every little thing is
gonna be all right.

—Bob Marley

JUNE 5

A bit of fragrance clings to the hand
that gives flowers.

—Chinese proverb

Follow every rainbow, Till you find your dream.

—Rodgers and Hammerstein

Life moves forward. If
you keep looking back,
you won't be able to see
where you're going.

—Charles Carroll

The only person
you are destined to
become is the person
you decide to be.

—Ralph Waldo Emerson

One of the
secrets of life
is that all that is
really worth the
doing is what we
do for others.

—Lewis Carroll

Whether you believe you
can or believe you can't,
you are absolutely right.

—Henry Ford

Fall seven times.
Stand up eight.

—Japanese proverb

The most beautiful thing
we can experience is
the mysterious. It is the
source of all true art
and science.

—Albert Einstein

Be humble, for you are
made of earth.
Be noble, for you are
made of stars.

—Serbian proverb

In a gentle
way, you can
shake the
world.

—Mahatma Gandhi

We do not ask for what useful
purpose the birds do sing, for
song is their pleasure
since they were created for
singing. Similarly, we ought
not to ask why the human
mind troubles to fathom the
secrets of the heavens. . . .

—Johannes Kepler

—Clare

Even if you don't win, listen to the small voice inside of you that says you are always a winner.

—Josh

When we know how to read our
own hearts, we acquire wisdom
of the hearts of others.

—Denis Diderot

Let me not pray to be sheltered from dangers but to be fearless in facing them.

—Rabindranath Tagore

Thank you to life that has
given me so much.
It's given me the strength
of my weary feet,
With which I have walked
through cities and puddles,
Beaches and deserts,
Mountains and plains. . . .

—Violeta Parra, "Gracias a la Vida"

The greatest danger for
most of us is not that our
aim is too high and we
miss it, but that it is too
low and we reach it.

—Michelangelo Buonarroti

He who
travels has
stories to
tell.

—Gaelic proverb

Courage is found in
unlikely places.

—J.R.R. Tolkien

Every day, in every way, I'm getting better and better.

—Émile Coué

JUNE 25

Sail the ocean
even when others stay
on the shore.

—Emma

LIFE IS NOT COLORFUL.

LIFE IS

COLORING

—Paco

The true secret of happiness lies in taking a genuine interest in all the details of daily life.

—William Morris

How many things are looked upon as quite impossible until they have actually been effected?

—Pliny the Elder

Kindness is
like snow.
It beautifies
everything
it covers.

—Kahlil Gibran

Every day

may not

be glorious,

but there's something

glorious in

every day.

Find the glory!

—Caleb

I have to admit, I love getting postcard precepts in the summer. Some of them come on real postcards. Others come as part of longer letters, like this one:

Dear Mr. Browne,
　　Here's my precept: "If you can get through middle school without hurting anyone's feelings, that's really cool beans."
　　I hope you are having a super-nice summer! My mom and I went to visit Auggie's family in Montauk on July 4th! They had fireworks on the beach! PLUS—there was a telescope on his roof! Every night I got to go up and look at the stars! Did I ever tell you that I want to be an astronomer when I grow up? I know all the constellations by heart. I also know a lot about the science of stars. For instance, do you know what stars are made of? Maybe you do because you're a teacher, but a lot of people don't. A star is pretty much just a giant cloud of hydrogen and helium gases. When it gets old, it starts to shrink, which kind of creates all these other elements. And then when all the elements get so tiny they can't go anywhere, they explode and send all their stardust into the universe! *That* dust is what forms planets and moons and mountains—and even people! Isn't that so awesome? We're all made of stardust!

　　　　　　　　　Love,
　　　　　　　　　Summer Dawson

Yep, I sure do love my job. As long as little kids like Summer keep reaching for the stars, I'll be here to cheer them on.

　　　　　　　　　　　　　　—Mr. Browne

JULY

Practice random kindness and senseless acts of beauty.

—Anne Herbert

Don't be afraid to take a big step. You can't cross a chasm in two small jumps.

—David Lloyd George

It is always easier to
fight for one's principles
than to live up to them.

—Alfred Adler

Great works are performed
not by strength but by
perseverance.

—Samuel Johnson

Shoot for the moon, because
even if you miss, you'll land
among the stars.

—Les Brown

Life is not
measured by
the number
of breaths we
take, but by
the moments
that take our
breath away.

—Unknown

Greatness lies not in being strong, but in the right using of strength.

—Henry Ward Beecher

Shall we make a new rule
of life from tonight: always to
try to be a little kinder than
is necessary?

—J. M. Barrie

—Buddha

There's only one corner
of the universe you can be
certain of improving, and
that's your own self.

—Aldous Huxley

At the end of the game,
pawns and kings go back
into the same box.

—Italian proverb

To the world,
You are one person.
But to one person,
You may be the
WORLD!

—Unknown

Each of us
has his own
alphabet
with which
to create
poetry.

—Irving Stone

If something stands
to be gained, nothing
will be lost.

—Miguel de Cervantes

Determination is
the wake-up call
to the human will.

—Anthony Robbins

The sun'll come out

tomorrow.

—*Annie* (Martin Charnin)

Ride on! Rough-shod
if need be, smooth-shod if
that will do, but ride on!
Ride on over all obstacles,
and win the race!

—Charles Dickens

The best things in life are not things.

—Ginny Moore

Tomorrow to
fresh woods, and
pastures new.

—John Milton

If you want
to learn about
the world
go out in it.

—Mae

You miss
100 percent
of the shots
you don't take.

—Wayne Gretzky

Remember there's
no such thing as a
small act of kindness.
Every act creates a ripple
with no logical end.

—Scott Adams

SUCCESS

does not come through grades, degrees or distinctions. It comes through experiences that expand your belief in what is

POSSIBLE

—Matea

Believe you can and you're halfway there.

—Theodore Roosevelt

An age is called Dark not
because the light fails to
shine but because people
fail to see it.

—James Michener

There is no wealth but life.

—John Ruskin

You're never
a loser until
you quit trying.

—Mike Ditka

Return to old watering
holes for more than
water; friends and dreams
are there to meet you.

—African proverb

The beauty of a living thing
is not the atoms that go
into it, but the way those
atoms are put together.

—Carl Sagan

THOSE WHO >>>> bring SUNSHINE TO THE LIVES OF others CANNOT KEEP IT FROM THEMSELVES

—J. M. Barrie

We must be willing

to let go of the life

we have planned, so

as to have the life

that is waiting for us.

—E. M. Forster

S ometimes people surprise you. You think you have
them figured out, but they'll do something that
makes you realize just how fathomless the human heart
truly is. To that end, and because the heart of a child
is still such a work in progress, no one can surprise
you more than a child. This happened to me over the
course of a recent email exchange with a former student. This kid did not have a great year in fifth grade.
Most of it was his own doing: he made bad choices. He
was something of a bully, and the tide turned against
him, as it should have. He found that his small-minded
dislikes weren't as universal as he thought, and that he
was alone in his prejudices.

However, I always suspected that there was a little bit more to this boy than that. His personal essays
betrayed a more feeling heart than his actions implied.
At times, it was hard to reconcile the boy who could be
so hateful with the boy who wrote the essays. So I held
out hope for him. And when I got an email from him
over the summer, I couldn't have been happier.

To: tbrowne@beecherschool.edu
Fr: julianalbans@ezmail.com
Re: My precept

Hi, Mr. Browne! I just sent you my precept in
the mail: "SOMETIMES IT'S GOOD TO START
OVER." It's on a postcard of a gargoyle. I wrote

this precept because I'm going to a new school in September. I ended up hating Beecher Prep. I didn't like the students. But I DID like the teachers. I thought your class was great. So don't take my not going back personally.

I don't know if you know the whole long story, but basically the reason I'm not going back to Beecher Prep is . . . well, not to name names, but there was one student I really didn't get along with. Actually, it was two students. (You can probably guess who they are.) Anyway, these kids were not my favorite people in the world. We started writing mean notes to each other. I repeat: *each other.* It was a 2-way street! But I'm the one who got in trouble for it! Just me! It was so unfair! The truth is, Mr. Tushman had it in for me because my mom was trying to get him fired. Anyway, long story short: I got suspended for two weeks for writing the notes! (No one knows this, though. It's a secret, so please don't tell anyone.) The school said it had a "zero tolerance" policy against bullying. But I don't think what I did was bullying! My parents got so mad at the school! They decided to enroll me in a different school next year. So, yeah, that's the story.

I really wish that "student" had never come to Beecher Prep! My whole year would have been so much better! I hated having to be in his classes. He gave me nightmares. I would still be going to Beecher Prep if he hadn't been there. It's a bummer.

I really liked your class, though. You were a
great teacher. I wanted you to know that.

To: julianalbans@ezmail.com
Fr: tbrowne@beecherschool.edu
Re: Re: My precept

Hi, Julian. Thanks so much for your email! I'm
looking forward to getting the gargoyle postcard.
I was sorry to hear you won't be coming back
to Beecher Prep. I always thought you were a
great student and a gifted writer.
     By the way, I love your precept. I agree,
sometimes it's good to start over. A fresh start
gives us the chance to reflect on the past, weigh
the things we've done, and apply what we've
learned from those things to the way we move
forward. If we don't examine the past, we don't
learn from it.
     As for the "kids" you didn't like, I do think
I know who you're talking about. I'm sorry
the year didn't turn out to be a happy one for
you, but I hope you take a little time to ask
yourself why. Things that happen to us, even
the bad stuff, can often teach us a little bit
about ourselves. Do you ever wonder why you
had such a hard time with these two students?
Was it, perhaps, their friendship that bothered
you? Were you troubled by Auggie's physical
appearance? You mentioned that you started
having nightmares. Sometimes fear can make
even the nicest kids say and do things they

wouldn't ordinarily say or do. Perhaps you should explore these feelings further?

In any case, I wish you the best of luck in your new school, Julian. You're a good kid. A natural leader. Just remember to use your leadership for good, huh? Don't forget: always choose kind!

To: tbrowne@beecherschool.edu
Fr: julianalbans@ezmail.com
Re: Re: Re: My precept

Thanks so much for your email, Mr. Browne! It really made me feel good! Like, you really "get" me. And you don't think I'm a bad kid, which is nice. I feel like everyone thinks I'm this "demon child." It's nice to know you don't.

I had begun to read your email and my grandmother saw me smiling so she asked me to read it aloud to her. Grandmère is French. I'm staying with her in Paris for the summer. So I read it to her. And we got into this whole long talk after. Grandmère's old, but she's still kind of with it. And anyway, guess what? She totally agreed with you! She thinks maybe I was kind of mean to Auggie because I was a little afraid of him. And after talking to her about it, I think maybe you guys are right. The thing about the nightmares I was having is that I used to get bad nightmares when I was little. Night terrors. Anyway, I hadn't had one in a long time, but the first time I saw Auggie in Mr. Tushman's office,

I started having them again. It sucked! It actually made me not want to go to school because I didn't want to see his face again!

I know I would have had a better year if Auggie had never come to Beecher Prep. But I know it's not his fault that he looks the way he does. My grandmother told me this long story about a boy she knew when she was a girl, and how kids used to be mean to him. It made me feel so sorry for him! It made me feel bad about some of the things I said to Auggie.

So anyway, I wrote Auggie a note. I don't have his address, though, so can I mail it to you so that you could mail it to Auggie? I don't know how much the stamp costs, but I'll totally pay you back. (It's a nice note, btw! Don't worry!)

Thanks again, Mr. Browne. Seriously. Thanks!

To: julianalbans@ezmail.com
Fr: tbrowne@beecherschool.edu
Re: Proud!

Julian, I can't tell you how proud I am that you've taken this big step! I would be honored to mail that note to Auggie for you when I get it (and you don't have to worry about paying me back for the stamp). Looks like you're really living up to your precept. Good for you, Julian!

Look, the truth is, it's not easy coping with fear. In fact, it's one of the hardest things human beings have to face. That's because fear isn't always rational. Do you know the origin of fear? It goes back to the dawn of mankind. When we were pre-humans, we developed fear as a mechanism to survive in a tough world— poisonous snakes and spiders, saber-toothed cats, wolves. The instinctual response to a perceived danger would trigger adrenaline inside us, and we could run away faster, or fight better, in response to that perceived danger. It's a very natural instinct, Julian. To be afraid is one of the things that make us human.

But another thing that makes us human is our ability to deal with fear. We have other traits that we rely on that help us cope with our fears. The ability to be courageous despite our fear. The ability to regret. The ability to feel. The ability to be kind. These traits work together, along with fear, to make us better people.

Next year is going to be a great year for you, Julian. I can feel it. I have faith in you! Just give everyone a chance and you'll do fine. Best of luck to you!

Sometimes, all a kid needs is a little push to have a revelation. I'm not saying I was that push. I think Julian's very wise grandmother was. The point is: everyone's got a story. The challenge with some kids is to be patient enough to listen.

—Mr. Browne

AUGUST

That is the
beginning of
knowledge—
the discovery of
something we do
not understand.

—Frank Herbert

Far away in the sunshine are
my highest aspirations.
I may not reach them, but
I can look up and see their
beauty, believe in them, and
try to follow where they lead.

—Louisa May Alcott

Just as there is no loss of basic energy in the universe, so no thought or action is without its effects, present or ultimate, seen or unseen, felt or unfelt.

—Norman Cousins

I am part of all that I have met.

—Alfred, Lord Tennyson

Do not seek to follow in the footsteps of the wise. Seek what they sought.

—Matsuo Bashō

Courage doesn't
always roar.
Sometimes
courage is the
quiet voice at the
end of the
day saying,
"I will try
again tomorrow."

—Mary Anne Radmacher

The more
I wonder,
the more
I love.

—Alice Walker

You can never
cross the ocean
unless you have
the courage
to lose sight of
the shore.

—André Gide

One of the most essential
prerequisites to happiness is
unbounded tolerance.

—A. C. Fifield

You don't get
harmony when
everyone
sings the
same note.

—Doug Floyd

ALWAYS BE ON
THE LOOKOUT FOR
THE PRESENCE
OF WONDER.

—E. B. White

Life is not meant to be easy, my child; but take courage: it can be delightful.

—George Bernard Shaw

I cannot do all the
good that the world
needs, but the
world needs all the
good that I can do.

—Jana Stanfield

—Unknown

The splendid achievements
of the intellect, like the soul,
are everlasting.

—Sallust

The sage has
one advantage:
He is immortal.
If this is not his
century, many
others will be.

—Baltasar Gracián

THE THINGS THAT MAKE ME DIFFERENT ARE THE THINGS THAT MAKE ME **ME**.

—Piglet (A. A. Milne)

We measure minds by their stature; it would be better to estimate them by their beauty.

—Joseph Joubert

It always seems
impossible until
it is done.

—Nelson Mandela

A wise man can
learn more from
a foolish
question than a
fool can learn from
a wise answer.

—Bruce Lee

If you want to go quickly,
go alone. If you want to go far,
go together.

—African proverb

A STUMBLE MAY PREVENT A FALL.

—English proverb

Whatever is worth doing at all
is worth doing well.

—Philip Dormer Stanhope

Yesternight the
sun went hence,
And yet is here
today.

—John Donne

Kindness, like a boomerang,
always returns.

—Unknown

Just keep swimming no matter how hard the current.

—Ava

Wisdom is like a
baobab tree:
No one person can
embrace it, but
a tribe can.

—African proverb

The butterfly counts not
months but moments, and
has time enough.

—Rabindranath Tagore

AUGUST 29

A good
name will
shine forever.

—African proverb

Very little is
needed to make
a happy life.

—Marcus Aurelius

Nothing in Nature is unbeautiful.

—Alfred, Lord Tennyson

GLITTER

Kindness can spread from person to person like glitter. Anyone who's ever introduced glitter into any kind of art project at school knows exactly of what I speak. You can't shake it off you. You pass it on to the next person. Its sparkling remnants linger for days. And for each tiny dot you find, you know that a hundred more have seemingly vanished. But where did they go? What happens to all that glitter?

I had a boy in my class last year whose name was August. He was quite special, and not because of his face. There was just something about his indomitable spirit that captured me (and a lot of the people around him). The year turned out to be a raging success for Auggie. I was very glad about that. Now, I'm not naive enough to think that a happy ending to a fifth-grade year will guarantee him a happy life. I know he'll have more than his share of challenges. But what I gleaned from his triumphant year was this: he has what he needs inside of him to stand up to life's challenges. Auggie will have a beautiful life. That's my prediction.

I got an email from him the other day that kind of validates this prediction.

To: tbrowne@beecherschool.edu
Fr: apullman@beecherschool.edu
Re: The postcard

Hey there, Mr. Browne! Long time no speak!

I hope you're having a great summer! I sent you my precept last month. Hope you got it. It had a giant fish on it. From Montauk.

So I'm writing to thank you for sending me Julian's note in the mail. Whoa, I did not see that coming! When I opened your letter I was, like, what is this other envelope? And then I opened it and I saw the handwriting. And I was like, no way, is Julian sending me mean notes again? You probably don't know this, but Julian left some really mean notes in my locker last year. Anyway, it turned out that this note wasn't a mean note! It was actually an apology! Can you believe it? It was sealed, so maybe you didn't read it, but this is what the note said:

DEAR AUGGIE,

I WANT TO APOLOGIZE FOR THE STUFF I DID LAST YEAR. I'VE BEEN THINKING ABOUT IT A LOT. YOU DIDN'T DESERVE IT. I WISH I COULD HAVE A DO-OVER. I WOULD BE NICER. I HOPE YOU DON'T REMEMBER HOW MEAN I WAS WHEN YOU'RE EIGHTY YEARS OLD. HAVE A NICE LIFE.

—JULIAN

PS: IF YOU'RE THE ONE WHO TOLD MR. TUSHMAN ABOUT THE NOTES, DON'T WORRY, I'M NOT MAD.

I'm kind of in a state of shock about this note. By the way, he's wrong about me being the one who told Mr. Tushman. It wasn't me (or Summer or Jack). Maybe Mr. Tushman really does have microscopic spy satellites tracking everything we do in school! Maybe he's even watching me . . . right NOW! If you're listening, Mr. Tushman, I hope you had a great summer! Anyway, just goes to show, you never know with people!

To: apullman@beecherschool.edu
Fr: tbrowne@beecherschool.edu
Re: Re: The postcard

Hey there, Auggie (and Mr. Tushman, if you're listening). I just wanted to write you a quick little note to say how happy I am that you got some closure with Julian. There's nothing that can make up for what he put you through, but there must be some satisfaction in knowing that he's grown as a person because of you. You're right: you just never know with people! See you next month!

To: tbrowne@beecherschool.edu
Fr: apullman@beecherschool.edu
Re: The truth revealed?

Yeah, it's true. You never know! I showed my mom the postcard and she just about fainted. "Will wonders never cease!" she said. Then I told Jack and he was like, "Did you check the postcard for poison?" You know Jack. But seriously, I don't know what might have motivated Julian to write the apology, but I really appreciated it. The one thing I still don't know is: WHO TOLD MR. TUSHMAN ABOUT THE NOTES? Was it you, Mr. Browne?

To: apullman@beecherschool.edu
Fr: tbrowne@beecherschool.edu
Re: Re: The truth revealed?

Ha! I promise, it wasn't me who told Mr. Tushman. I had no idea about those awful notes! It may just be one of those mysteries that never get solved!

To: tbrowne@beecherschool.edu
Fr: apullman@beecherschool.edu
Re: Re: The truth revealed?

So here's the thing about glitter: once it's out of the bottle, there's just no way of putting it back. It's the same with kindness. Once it pours out of your soul, there's no way of containing it. It just continues to spread from person to person, a shining, sparkling, wonderful thing.

—Mr. Browne

SEPTEMBER

When given the choice between being right or being kind, choose kind.

—Dr. Wayne W. Dyer

Begin, be bold, and venture to be wise.

—Horace

SEPTEMBER 3

The wisest men
follow their own
course.

—Euripides

Life isn't about
finding yourself.
Life is about
creating yourself.

—George Bernard Shaw

Beauty is not in the face; beauty is a light in the heart.

—Kahlil Gibran

The secret of
getting things
done is to act!

—Dante Alighieri

Accept what you
can't change.
Change what you
can't accept.

—Unknown

SEPTEMBER 8

You can't have

a rainbow

without

a little bit

of Rain

—Unknown

An act of kindness never dies,
but extends the invisible
undulations of its influence
over the breadth of centuries.

—Father Faber

If there is no struggle, there is no progress.

—Frederick Douglass

Every hour of
the light and DARK
is a miracle.

—Walt Whitman

Never hesitate to tell the
truth. And never, ever give
in or give up.

—Bella Abzug

Find beauty in the world, and the world will find beauty in you.

—Zöe

Sometimes rejection in life is really redirection.

—Tavis Smiley

I don't believe you have to be
better than everybody else.
I believe you have to be better
than you thought you could be.

—Ken Venturi

Being nice is being cool !

—Alexis

What is a friend?
A single soul dwelling
in two bodies.

—Aristotle

Sometimes
the questions
are complicated
but the
answers
are simple.

—Dr. Seuss

You are a conductor
of light.

—Sir Arthur Conan Doyle

Knowledge is love
and light and vision.

—Helen Keller

Strong people don't put others down. They lift them up.

—Michael P. Watson

To him whose elastic and vigorous thought keeps pace with the sun, the day is a perpetual morning.

—Henry David Thoreau

I believe that unarmed truth
and unconditional love will
have the final word.

—Martin Luther King, Jr.

Treat others
how you
want to be
treated.

—Proverb

Nothing happens unless first a dream.

—Carl Sandburg

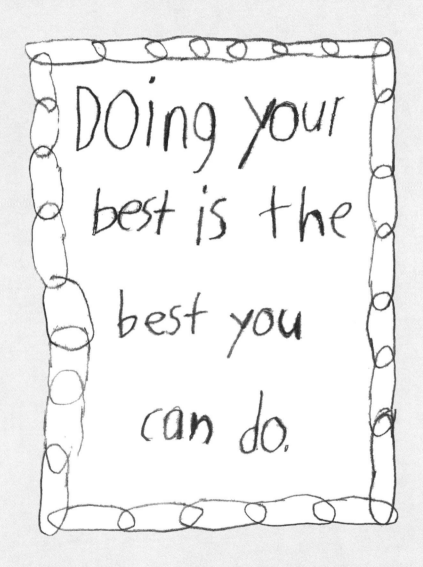

DOing your best is the best you can do.

—Riley

Come forth into the light
of things. Let Nature be
your teacher.

—William Wordsworth

Ah! the immensity of the value of persons to each other, and of kind deeds and affectionate inventions between them, for the making of happiness!

—James Vila Blake, *More Than Kin*

You are
your own
little light,
shine bright
so everyone
can see.

—Elizabeth

There are always flowers
for those who want to
see them.

—Henri Matisse

I've always thought that good teaching is about illumination. Sure, we teach things kids might not know, but a lot of the time, we're just shedding light on the stuff they already do know. There's a lot of that happening in the fifth grade. Kids know how to read, but I'm trying to get them to *love* reading. Kids know how to write, but I'm trying to inspire them to express themselves better. In both instances, they have the materials they need already inside them: I'm just here to guide them a bit, to shed a little light. To illume.

That's one of the reasons I like to start every year off with the Dr. Wayne W. Dyer precept about "choosing kind." The kids are all new to middle school. A lot of them don't know each other. I think of this precept as a preemptive strike against much of what is to come, an inception in their psyches. I plant a little notion of kindness so that at least it's there, this seedling buried inside them. Will it take root? Will it flower? Who knows? But either way, I've done my deed.

When given the choice between being right or being kind, choose kind.

—Dr. Wayne W. Dyer

This particular quote usually provokes days of discussion after I introduce it. I often start my conversation about precepts with a general survey: Do you like the precept? Does it apply to how you live your life? What do you think it means?

Then I start talking about the obvious benefits of the precept. If everyone adopted that quote as his or her own personal precept, I ask them, wouldn't the world be a better place? Imagine if nations adopted it as a mandate—wouldn't there be fewer conflicts? Some kids agree, adding that if nations chose to be kind instead of right, it might even end world hunger. Other kids argue that being wealthy doesn't have anything to do with being right.

I sometimes ask the students how hard it would be for them to choose to back down from an argument with their moms or dads or siblings if they knew they were right and the other person was wrong. Would they give in just to let the other person save face? Why? Why not? This part of the discussion is often *very* lively!

It's not so simple a thing to choose to be kind. It's one thing to back down from an argument with someone you love—a friend, say—because you don't see the point in "winning" the argument at the cost of your friend's feelings. But what if you believe in something that no one else believes in? What if you're the only one who knows you're right? Should you back down, just to be kind? What if you were Galileo and you knew you were right about the planets revolving around the sun, even though the rest of the world thought you were crazy—would you back down? What if you were living in the 1950s and you were against segregation—would you back down, just to be polite? What if you were standing up for something you believed in—would you really want to back down, just for the sake of kindness? No! You'd stand up and fight, right?

All this will often lead to some kids questioning whether the precept is really good, after all. At this point, I always suggest to them that maybe the most important words in the precept aren't "kind" or "right." Maybe the most important word in that whole sentence is the word "choose." You have the choice. What do you choose?

As I said, my job is to plant the notion in your minds, kids. Inception. Once the seed is planted, all I try to do is keep shedding some light on it. And watch it grow. In time, you'll begin shining your own lights, and then—watch out, world!

—Mr. Browne

OCTOBER

Your deeds are your monuments.

—Inscription on an Egyptian tomb

I do not believe in a fate that falls on men however they act; but I do believe in a fate that falls on them unless they act.

—G. K. Chesterton

It is better to be in
the dark with a friend
than to be in the light
without one.

—John

What you do
every day
matters more
than what you
do every once
in a while.

—Unknown

Don't Cry
because it's
OVER,
smile
because
IT happened.

—Dr. Seuss

Be bold enough to use your
voice, brave enough to listen
to your heart, and strong
enough to live the life
you've always imagined.

—Unknown

Great opportunities
to help others seldom
come, but small ones
surround us every day.

—Sally Koch

INVITE OTHERS TO
WONDER WITH YOU.

—Austin Kleon, *Steal Like an Artist*

Kindness is the golden chain by which society is bound together.

—Johann Wolfgang von Goethe

If you can't change your
fate, change your attitude.

—Amy Tan

Rise above the little things.

—John Burroughs

Inward happiness almost always follows a kind action.

—Father Faber

I ask not for a lighter burden, but for broader shoulders.

—Jewish proverb

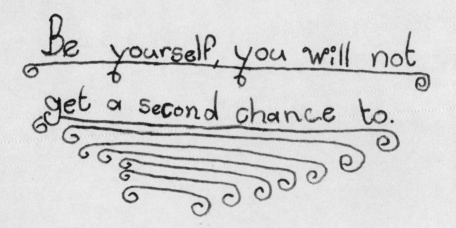

Be yourself, you will not get a second chance to.

—Daniel

Love truth, but pardon error.

—Voltaire

What makes night within us may leave stars.

—Victor Hugo

Normal is a setting

on a washing machine.

—Unknown

The best angle from which to approach any problem is the try-angle.

—Unknown

Don't choose the one who is beautiful to the world. But rather, choose the one who makes your world beautiful.

—Harry Styles

Seek not,
my soul,
immortal life,
but make the
most of what is
within thy reach.

—Pindar

We make our world
significant by the courage of
our questions and the depth
of our answers.

—Carl Sagan

Fashion your life as a garden of beautiful deeds.

—Unknown

Be kind, for everyone you meet is fighting a hard battle.

—Ian Maclaren

The soul aids the body, and at certain
moments, raises it. It is the only bird
which bears up its own cage.

—Victor Hugo

Everything has its wonders,
even darkness and silence,
and I learn, whatever state I
am in, therein to be content.

—Helen Keller

It is only with the
heart that one can
see rightly; what is
essential is invisible
to the eye.

—Antoine de Saint Exupéry

Even the darkest hour has

only sixty minutes.

—Morris Mandel

The mind is everything. What you think you become.

—Unknown

Constant kindness can
accomplish much.
As the sun makes ice
melt, kindness causes
misunderstanding, mistrust,
and hostility to evaporate.

—Albert Schweitzer

Find out what
your gift is,
and nurture it.

—Katy Perry

The way to have a
friend is to be a friend.

—Hugh Black

I read an article a few years ago about a couple of biologists who studied a troop of baboons over a twenty-year period. This particular troop was full of very aggressive "alpha" male baboons that routinely attacked and bullied the females and weaker males in the troop, depriving them of access to food sources. This proved unexpectedly advantageous one day when the alpha males ate infected meat. They all died, but the females and weaker males survived. Within a short time, the baboon troop took on a totally new dynamic. They were significantly less aggressive, more social, and, behaviorally, less "stressed" than before. What's more, these changes lasted long after that first generation of "nicer" baboons died out. New baboons joining the troop assimilated the less aggressive behavior and passed it on. The transmission of "kindness"—if such it could be called—took root. And it grew.

So, why am I talking about baboons? No, I'm not about to compare a class of fifth graders to baboons, don't worry! But I *am* going to go out on a limb (ha, no pun intended) and draw the following lesson: a small, dominant clique can set the tone for a group. Ask any teacher. If you're lucky enough to have a few alpha kids in your class who can set a positive tone for the year, you're in for a good year. Conversely, if you happen to get a few dominant kids who are bent on making trouble, then fasten your seat belts!

Last year turned out to be a great year. Although the usual fifth-grade antics were intensified by the

Auggie and Julian "rift," which ended well for Auggie, there was little drama among the girls. Summer, with her self-confident, sprightly nature, was a great influence. I had another student, Charlotte, who was also very sweet. We had this exchange via Google Docs the other day:

Hi, Mr. Browne. I'm writing an article for the school newspaper and was wondering if I could interview you about precepts. Hope you have the time.

Hi, Charlotte. I'd be happy to help.

Oh yay! Thank you! First of all, did you get my precept over the summer? "It's not enough to be friendly. You have to be a friend."

Yes, I did! Thank you for sending it. I liked it very much.

Thanks! You're probably wondering why I chose that precept.

Yes, actually. I'm very curious.

Oh, well, here's why. Do you remember at graduation, how Auggie won the Beecher Award? I thought that was so cool because he really deserved it. But I also kind of thought that other people should have won it, too. Like Jack. And Summer. They were such good friends to Auggie—even in the beginning, when kids were running away from him.

Hey, this part isn't going to be in the newspaper, right?

Totally not!

Just checking! Sorry to interrupt.

No prob. It's just that I started thinking about how I had never really gotten to know Auggie myself. Like, I was nice to him. I said hello in the hallways. I was never mean to him. But, you know, I never did what Summer did. I never sat down with him at lunchtime. I never defended him to my friends, like Jack did.

Don't be too hard on yourself, Charlotte. You were always very nice.

Yeah, but "being nice" is not the same as "choosing kind."

I see your point.

This year, I started sitting at the "summer" table. It's me, Auggie, Summer, Jack, Maya, and Reid. I know some kids still don't like being around Auggie, but that's their problem, right?

Very right.

So anyway, back to the newspaper article. I was wondering if you could share with readers why you first started collecting precepts? What inspired you?

Hmm. I guess I first came upon the notion of collecting precepts when I was in college. I happened upon the writings of Sir Thomas Browne, a seventeenth-century man of all trades, and found his work deeply moving.

Seriously? His name was Thomas Browne?

Incredible coincidence, isn't it?

So when did you start teaching precepts to kids?

Not too long afterward, when I started student teaching. Actually, it's funny that you're asking me these questions, because I've been thinking about putting together a book of all the precepts I've collected over the years, along with some essays in which I touch upon some of the very questions you're asking me.

Really? That is such an awesome idea! I would totally buy that book!

Good! I'm glad you like it.

So I think those were the only questions I had. I'm looking forward to reading your book when it comes out.

Thank you. Bye, Charlotte!

What I loved most about this exchange was the idea that Charlotte herself realized the profound impact of kindness.

I began this essay with a true story of baboons, and ended with the story of a girl. In both, the transmission of kindness had taken root. What can biologists and teachers alike do but marvel at its impact?

—Mr. Browne

NOVEMBER

Have no friends not
equal to yourself.

—Confucius

It is a rough road that leads to the heights of greatness.

—Seneca

No one is good
at everything
but everyone
is good at
something.

—Clark

Turn your wounds
into wisdom.

—Oprah Winfrey

In kindness is encompassed
every variety of wisdom.

—Ernesto Sábato

Don't strive for love, be it.

—Hugh Prather

Good friends are like stars.
You don't always see them,
but you know they're
always there.

—Unknown

When life
gives you
lemons,
make orange
juice.
Be unique!

—J.J.

If opportunity doesn't knock, build a door.

—Milton Berle

O world, I am in tune
with every note of
thy great harmony.

—Marcus Aurelius

My religion is
very simple.
My religion is
kindness.

—Dalai Lama

Today, fill
your cup of
life with
sunshine and
laughter.

—Dodinsky

Life is like sailing. You can
use any wind to go
in any direction.

—Robert Brault

If you're lucky
enough to be different,
don't ever change.

—Taylor Swift

If costs nothing

To be nice.

—Harry Styles

To succeed in life, you need
three things: a wishbone,
a backbone and a funny bone.

—Reba McEntire

The devotion of
thought to an honest
achievement makes the
achievement possible.

—Mary Baker Eddy

When you are living the
best version of yourself, you
inspire others to live the
best versions of themselves.

—Steve Maraboli

The happiness of life is made up of minute fractions—the little, soon forgotten charities of a kiss or smile, a kind look, a heartfelt compliment, and the countless infinitesimals of pleasurable and genial feeling.

—Samuel Taylor Coleridge

If you don't know, you should ask.

—Hailey

TO *Love* ANOTHER PERSON IS TO SEE THE FACE OF GOD

—*Les Misérables, The Musical* (Alain Boublil)

Kindness can become its own motive. We are made kind by being kind.

—Eric Hoffer

What this
world needs
is a new
kind of
army—the
army of the
kind.

—Cleveland Amory

Let us be grateful to people
who make us happy. They are
the charming gardeners who
make our souls blossom.

—Marcel Proust

And the song, from
beginning to end,
I found again in the
heart of a friend.

—Henry Wadsworth Longfellow

Happiness is a perfume
you cannot pour on
others without getting a
few drops on yourself.

—Unknown

Good deeds can lead to more good deeds which can lead to more good deeds that will eventually lead back to you!

—Nicolas

There are no shortcuts to
any place worth going.

—Beverly Sills

WHEN IT'S DARK, BE THE ONE WHO

TURNS

ON

THE

LIGHT.

—Joseph

Big shots are only
little shots who
keep shooting.

—Christopher Morley

One of my students dressed up as Frodo for Halloween last month, which caused me to casually make this offhand remark: "I love Frodo, but, let's face it, Samwise Gamgee is the greatest hero of Middle-earth."

Well, you would have thought I'd just said we were doing away with Halloween or something, judging from the number of gasps and "No way!"s I got. I don't remember the last time one of my statements generated so much controversy in my classroom! Although the class was more or less evenly split between Aragorn and Frodo as the greatest hero—with some Gandalf advocates—not one person agreed with me about Samwise.

So I tried to elaborate on my crazy thinking. Sam, I reminded them, was the loyal companion to Frodo through thick and thin. All those times Frodo was about to give up, Sam kept him going. When Frodo couldn't carry the ring anymore, Sam took Frodo on his back across the desolate plains of Mordor. When Sam thought Frodo was dead, he took the ring himself and set about to destroy it. And when the ring started working its seduction on him, Sam was one of the few creatures in all of Middle-earth who were able to resist the temptation. In a way, I told the kids, Sam stands as a shining example of the four virtues. In classical antiquity, it was believed that to be a truly great person, one should have in equal proportions the following four virtues:

WISDOM: prudence, as garnered from experience, or the ability to respond appropriately to any given situation.

JUSTICE: the ability to fight for what is right. The perpetual and constant will to render to each one his right.

COURAGE: the ability to confront fear, uncertainty, or intimidation.

TEMPERANCE: the ability to practice moderation—even when tempted to give in to one's own self-interest or desire. Temperance is the art of self-control.

Samwise Gamgee is the epitome of all those virtues, I told my students. But then they pointed out that he wasn't especially wise, which I had to give them. And he didn't really live for Justice, which I had to give them, too. Ultimately, we decided, as a whole, that Sam stood for Temperance. He never gave in to his own wishful thinking, but stood fast and firm to help his friends.

"So what other fictional heroes can we think of that stand for the other virtues?" I asked the kids. And this is where the fun began! I gave them a couple of days to do some research, and then we had our class discussion.

For Wisdom, the most common name offered was: Yoda. "Come on!" I rebuked in a comical way. "Really? That's such an obvious answer." I told them I thought the wisest character, if we were going the Star Wars route, was Luke Skywalker. Not at first, of course. But after Luke learned to master his own feelings and gained a deeper insight into others' feelings, he became a calm, cool, and collected Jedi Knight, who was smart enough to take on the dark side of the Force. They were not convinced. Apparently, Luke holds less appeal for the under-forty crowd than Yoda.

For Justice, we turned to The Chronicles of Narnia. Edmund, who actually becomes King Edmund the Just after redeeming himself, was the fairly unanimous choice.

For Courage, we went to the world of superheroes. A big debate arose about Superman versus Batman. Superman, it was pointed out, was very courageous, but then again, he was impervious to everything, except Kryptonite (and how many people carry Kryptonite in their pocket, right?). Batman, on the other hand, was just an ordinary guy with lots of gadgets, who was seriously brave. This remained an unresolved dispute, and just may be for the rest of time.

I actually used that great rivalry to bring up one of my all-time favorites: Achilles versus Hector. It was a fun way for me to introduce this ancient feud to those who hadn't heard about it. Basically, I told them, Achilles was the greatest hero of the Greeks. His mother was a goddess, and when he was a baby, she dunked him in the river Styx and made him invincible—except for his heel, which was where she was holding him. What's more, Achilles's armor was forged by a god, making him even more impossible to defeat. And to top it all off, Achilles was the best-trained warrior of all time: the dude liked to fight! Hector, on the other hand, who was the champion of the Trojans, did not like to fight. Nor did he have a goddess for a mother or a god to forge his armor. In fact, he was just an ordinary guy who was especially good with a sword, fighting to save his home when one thousand Greek ships invaded his shores.

Then I told the kids about the epic fight between Achilles and Hector. They were so excited by it! Who says kids can't be taught the classics anymore?

The final virtue to be debated was Temperance. What character from a book or movie best embodied the art of self-control? We turned to the world of Harry Potter for that one. Seems like Harry himself, though sometimes something of a rule-breaker, never abused his unique powers for self-gain. As one student said, he could have used his invisibility cloak a hundred times to do bad things, but he didn't. Instead, he used his powers for the greater good. That's the great lesson Rowling teaches.

It was quite a wonderful teaching day for me, one that sprang completely from a boy in a costume. Although I may have veered off-topic for a day, I think the lessons learned were more valuable than anything in today's curriculum.

Teachers need the freedom to teach—freedom they can't have if they're only teaching so their students can pass tests. I'm pretty sure my students won't find anything about Hector on the Common Core tests. I'm equally sure that what they learned about Wisdom, Justice, Courage, and Temperance may stay with them for the rest of their lives.

—Mr. Browne

DECEMBER

Fortune favors the bold.

—Virgil

Kindness is
difficult to give
away because
it keeps
coming back.

—Marcel Proust

The smallest
good deed is better
than the grandest
intention.

—Unknown

I'm not afraid of
storms, for I'm
learning how to sail
my ship.

—Louisa May Alcott

On that best portion of

a good man's life,

His little, nameless,

unremembered, acts

Of kindness and of love.

—William Wordsworth

By perseverance, the snail reached the ark.

—Charles Spurgeon

I believe that every human mind feels pleasure in doing good to another.

—Thomas Jefferson

I've learned
that life is like
a book. Some times
we must close a
chapter and begin
the next one.

—Hanz

You're like a bird,

spread your wings

and soar above

the clouds.

—Mairead

The sun does not
shine for a few trees
and flowers, but for
the wide world's joy

—Henry Ward Beecher

All our dreams can
come true—if we
have the courage to
pursue them.

—Walt Disney

Injustice anywhere is a threat
to justice everywhere.

—Martin Luther King, Jr.

You are never too old
to set another goal
or to dream a new
dream.

—C. S. Lewis

Life is like an ice-cream cone; you have to lick it one day at a time.

—Charles M. Schulz

Accept what you have
and treat it well.

—Brody

For beautiful eyes, look

for the good in others;

for beautiful lips, speak

only words of kindness;

and for poise, walk

with the knowledge

that you are never alone.

—Audrey Hepburn

True wisdom lies in
gathering the precious
things out of each day
as it goes by.

—E. S. Bouton

Nothing will work
unless you do.

—Maya Angelou

EVEN THE
SMALLEST
PERSON
CAN CHANGE
THE COURSE
OF THE FUTURE.

—J.R.R. Tolkien

To give service to a
single heart by a single act
is better than a thousand
heads bowing in prayer.

—Mahatma Gandhi

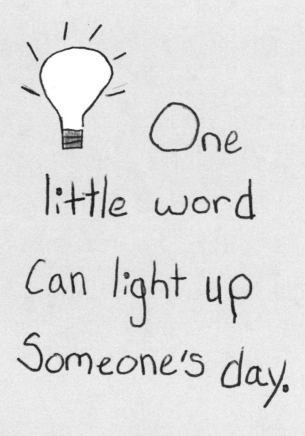

One little word can light up someone's day.

—Ainsley

Do your little bit of
good where you are;
it's those little bits of
good put together that
overwhelm the world.

—Desmond Tutu

Happiness resides
not in possessions,
and not in gold.
Happiness dwells
in the soul.

—Democritus

Goodness does not consist

in greatness, but greatness

in goodness.

—Athenaeus

A single sunbeam is enough to drive away many shadows.

—St. Francis of Assisi

Amid life's quests, there seems but worthy one: to do men good.

—Gamaliel Bailey

A big heart
is determined
to make other
hearts grow.

—Christina

Happiness is someone to love, something to do, and something to hope for.

—Chinese proverb

We didn't all come over on the same ship, but we're all in the same boat.

—Bernard Baruch

Dream your dreams,
but when you act,
plant your feet firmly on
the ground.

—Noel Clarasó

Let us always meet each other

with a smile. . . .

—Mother Teresa

MYSTERIES

December. The end of the year. The start of a new year. A chance to remember. A chance to look forward. It was nice hearing from some of my former students: Auggie. Summer. Charlotte. And, of course, the biggest surprise to me of all—Julian. That is, until I got this short and pithy email from Amos, one of my students from last year. This boy, who was generally a quiet kid, not one to speak up in class, surprised us all when he came to the rescue of Auggie and Jack at the nature retreat last year. He led the charge and showed great leadership. Sometimes kids don't even know they're leaders until they start to lead.

When I got this email, it was the answer to one little mystery (that I know I wasn't the only person to wonder about).

> To: tbrowne@beecherschool.edu
> Fr: amosconti@wazoomail.com
> Subject: My precept—at last!

Hey, Mr. B, hope you have a happy holiday! Sorry I didn't get around to sending you a postcard over the summer. Had a lot going on, you know? But here goes: "Don't try too hard to be cool. It always shows, and that's uncool."

What do you think? Cool, huh? I won't explain what my precept means because it's pretty obvious, right? I mean, you probably know who I'm talking about, right? Hee-hee-hee.

No, seriously. Last year was tough, man! Lots of drama! Yo, I'm not into drama, usually. That's why I was so sick and tired of that stuff going on with Julian. There's not a lot of drama this year, which is good. No one bothers Auggie anymore. I mean, a little, but not too much. Let's face it, people are always going to stare a bit. But Auggie's a tough little dude and no one messes with him anymore.

Okay, look, I'm going to let you in on a little secret. Ready? So, you know how Julian got in big trouble for leaving mean notes in Auggie's locker, right? Everyone says it's the real reason Julian's not coming back to school next year. I've even heard a few people say he was actually suspended for it! Anyway, the big mystery is: how did Mr. Tushman even find out about the notes? Auggie didn't tell him. Jack didn't tell him. Summer didn't tell him. Julian didn't tell him. Miles didn't tell him. And Henry didn't tell him. You know how I know? Because . . . drumroll here . . . it was me! I'm the one who told Mr. Tushman about the notes. Didn't see that coming, did you?

So let me explain a bit. What happened was that Henry and Miles knew Julian was leaving the mean notes. They told me about the notes but made me swear not to tell anyone. But after they told me, I thought it just really sucked big-time that Julian was being so mean to Auggie. It was kind of like bullying. And even though I swore to Henry and Miles that I wouldn't say anything, I needed to tell Tushman about it so he could do something to protect Auggie. Hey, I'm an upstander—not a bystander! Little dudes like Auggie need guys like me to step it up, right?

So that's the story, Mr. B. Don't go telling anyone, though! I don't want to be accused of being, you know, a "snitch." Then again, I guess I don't really care. I know I did the right thing.

Keep warm, Mr. B! It's cold out there!

Yeah, maybe it's cold out there, but this warmed my heart completely. I have to admit: I did not see that one coming. Just goes to show, everyone really does have a story to tell. And most people, at least in my experience, are a little more noble than they think they are.

—Mr. Browne

ACKNOWLEDGMENTS

So many people had a hand in making this book. I'd like to, first and foremost, acknowledge the amazing contribution of the children who sent in their precepts—whether they ended up being included in this volume or not. There were over 1,200 submissions from people all over the world. The ones included in this volume are the ones I thought represented the spirit of Mr. Browne's Precepts best. Precepts aren't just maxims or pretty quotes, after all—they are words to live by, to elevate the soul, that celebrate the goodness in people.

I'd also like to thank my husband, Russell, and our two sons, Caleb and Joseph, for helping me go through all the submissions, one by one, and for their wisdom, insight, support, and love in all matters. I couldn't do ANYTHING without you guys.

Thank you to Alyssa Eisner Henkin of Trident Media for being so incredible to work with on every level. Thank you to Erin Clarke, my WONDERful editor, Nancy Hinkel, Lauren Donovan, Judith Haut, Barbara Marcus, and the incredible team at Random House. A special thank-you to Janet Wygal, Diane João, and Artie Bennett for doing such an amazing job copyediting and helping me source so many of these quotes.

Thanks, as always, to the teachers and librarians who inspired me growing up, and who continue to inspire children every day. *You* are the real wonders of the world!

CONTRIBUTORS OF ORIGINAL PRECEPTS, ARTWORK, AND LETTERING

JANUARY 2: Roald Dahl quote contributed by Nate, age 10, Brooklyn, N.Y.

JANUARY 11: Paul Brandt quote contributed by Elia, age 13, Regina, Sask., Canada.

JANUARY 26: Oscar Wilde quote contributed by Faith, Greensboro, N.C.

JANUARY 31: Original precept by Dominic, Bennington, Vt.

FEBRUARY 4: Original precept by Madison, age 11, Port Jefferson, N.Y.

FEBRUARY 7: Original precept by Emily, age 11, Port Jefferson Station, N.Y.

FEBRUARY 10: Original precept by Rebecca, age 10, Troy, Mich.

FEBRUARY 13: Original precept by Lindsay, age 11, Troy, Mich.

FEBRUARY 16: Lloyd Jones quote contributed by Liam, age 13, Regina, Sask., Canada.

FEBRUARY 17: Original precept by Jack, age 11, Hudson, Mass.

FEBRUARY 23: Original precept by Shreya, age 10, Troy, Mich.

MARCH 5: Original precept by Antonio, age 11, San Ramon, Calif. Art by Joseph Gordon.

MARCH 7: Ralph Waldo Emerson quote contributed by Linh, age 13, Regina, Sask., Canada.

MARCH 13: Henry Stanley Haskins quote contributed by Deacon, age 12, Regina, Sask., Canada.

MARCH 18: Original precept by Cate, age 10, Nashville, Tenn.

MARCH 19: Original precept by Isabelle, age 10, Washington, D.C.

MARCH 21: Original precept by Matthew, age 11, Lanoka Harbor, N.J.

MARCH 22: Original precept by Thomas, St. George, Utah.

MARCH 24: Chinese proverb contributed by Nathan, age 13, Regina, Sask., Canada.

MARCH 25: Original precept by Ella, Bay Village, Ohio.

MARCH 31: Original precept by Kyler, age 10, Merrick, N.Y.

APRIL 5: Original precept by Delaney, age 10, Lanoka Harbor, N.J.

APRIL 6: Mahatma Gandhi quote contributed by Rosemary, age 10, Nashville, Tenn.

APRIL 11: Vince Lombardi quote contributed by Zachary, age 13, Regina, Sask., Canada.

APRIL 13: Original precept by Rory, age 11, Chicago, Ill.

APRIL 16: Ziggy quote contributed by Kate, age 11, Chicago, Ill.

APRIL 17: Artwork by Matthew, age 11, Jackson Heights, N.Y.

APRIL 19: Original precept by Anna, age 10, Glenview, Ill.

MAY 5: Vince Lombardi quote contributed by Emma, age 10, Dresden, Ohio.

MAY 7: Original precept by Grace, age 12, Croton-on-Hudson, N.Y.

MAY 14: Original precept by Dustin, Bennington, Vt.

MAY 16: Original precept by Gavin, age 10, Wilmette, Ill.

MAY 21: Original precept by Srishti, age 10, Troy, Mich.

MAY 27: Original precept by Flynn, age 10, Bowdoinham, Me.

MAY 28: Original precept by Madeline, age 11, Quebec, Canada.

JUNE 4: Bob Marley quote contributed by Angelina, age 11, Jackson Heights, N.Y.

JUNE 16: Original precept by Clare, age 11, State College, Penn.

JUNE 17: Original precept by Josh, age 10, Troy, Mich.

JUNE 25: Original precept by Emma, age 11, Croton-on-Hudson, N.Y.

JUNE 26: Original precept by Paco, age 26, Brazil.

JUNE 30: Original precept by Caleb, age 17, Brooklyn, N.Y.

JULY 12: Unknown precept contributed by Julia, age 10, Troy, Mich.

JULY 15: Anthony Robbins quote contributed by Cole, age 14, Regina, Sask., Canada.

JULY 20: Original precept by Mae, age 11, Marblehead, Mass.

JULY 23: Original precept by Matea, age 12, Regina, Sask., Canada.

AUGUST 5: Artwork by Ashley, age 11, Jackson Heights, N.Y.

AUGUST 10: Doug Floyd quote contributed by Abby, age 10, Merrick, N.Y.

AUGUST 26: Original precept by Ava, age 11, Blackstone, Mass.

AUGUST 30: Artwork by Ali, age 11, Jackson Heights, N.Y.

SEPTEMBER 8: Unknown precept contributed by Samantha, age 13, Regina, Sask., Canada.

SEPTEMBER 13: Original precept by Zöe, Greensboro, N.C.

SEPTEMBER 16: Original precept by Alexis, age 10, Quebec, Canada.

SEPTEMBER 24: Proverb contributed by Tayler, age 10, Dresden, Ohio.

SEPTEMBER 26: Original precept by Riley, age 10, St. George, Utah.

SEPTEMBER 29: Original precept by Elizabeth, age 9, Nashville, Tenn.

OCTOBER 3: Original precept by John, age 10, West Windsor, N.J.

OCTOBER 5: Dr. Seuss quote contributed by Katherine, Greensboro, N.C.

OCTOBER 14: Original precept by Daniel, age 12, Munich, Germany.

OCTOBER 22: Unknown precept contributed by Nate, age 10, Brooklyn, N.Y.

NOVEMBER 3: Original precept by Clark, age 12, Regina, Sask., Canada.

NOVEMBER 8: Original precept by J.J., Scotch Plains, N.J.

NOVEMBER 14: Taylor Swift quote contributed by Nikki, age 17, East Brunswick, N.J.

NOVEMBER 20: Original precept by Hailey, age 11, Chicago, Ill.

NOVEMBER 21: Les Misérables quote contributed by Katherine, age 11, San Diego, Calif.

NOVEMBER 27: Original precept by Nicolas, age 10, State College, Penn.

NOVEMBER 29: Original precept by Joseph, age 9, Brooklyn, N.Y.

DECEMBER 8: Original precept by Hanz, age 13, Regina, Sask., Canada.

DECEMBER 9: Original precept by Mairead, age 11, Franklin, Mass.

DECEMBER 13: C. S. Lewis quote contributed by Chidiadi, age 12, Regina, Sask., Canada.

DECEMBER 14: Charles M. Schulz quote contributed by Dani, age 14, East Brunswick, N.J.

DECEMBER 15: Original precept by Brody, age 10, Forked River, N.J.

DECEMBER 21: Original precept by Ainsley, age 10, Lakeview, N.Y.

DECEMBER 27: Original precept by Christina, El Paso, Tex.

DECEMBER 31: Original artwork: fox by Kevin, age 11, Jackson Heights, N.Y.; duck by Prasansha, age 11, Jackson Heights, N.Y.

Special thanks to Nikki Martinez, Dani Martinez, and Joseph Gordon for their help with additional art.

NOTE ON SOURCES: Every possible measure has been taken to ensure that the quotes in this book are attributed to their original sources. However, over the centuries, old maxims have had a way of resurfacing with variations in wording or different translations. For this book, where a famous quote or saying is commonly attributed to a specific person without dispute, the most common attribution is used, even if its original source cannot be verified. Where a quote is occasionally disputed, the attribution is credited as "unknown."